D0810719

"And after the virtual devastation of the American family, the rock upon which this country was founded, we are told that it takes a village—this is, the collective, and thus, the state—to raise a child. The state is now more involved than it has ever been in the raising of children, and children are now more neglected, abused, and mistreated than they have been in our time.

This is not a coincidence, and, with all due respect, I am here to tell you: it does not take a village to raise a child.

It takes a family."

Robert Dole
Republican Convention
San Diego 1996

$\mathcal{P}$resented to the_____family

$\mathcal{O}$n the occasion of

_____

$\mathcal{F}$rom

_____

$\mathcal{D}$ate

_____

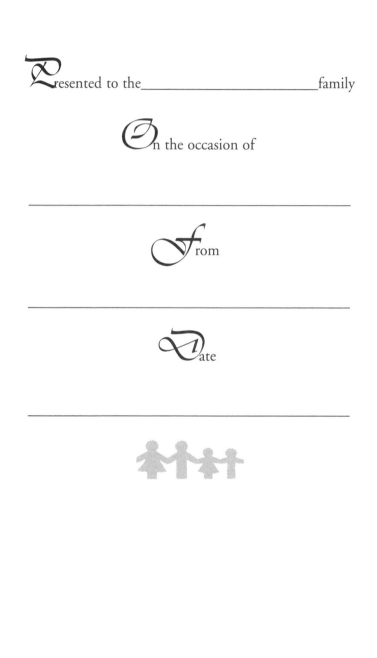

IT TAKES
a
FAMILY

Written and Illustrated by
Al Hartley

To Hermine
my decathlon wife
through whom God's blessings
flow and flow

ISBN 1-55748-946-7

Published by   Barbour & Company, Inc.
               P.O. Box 719
               Uhrichsville, Ohio 44683
               e-mail: books<barbour@tusco.net>

 Member of the
Evangelical Christian
Publishers Association

Printed in the United States of America.

Contents

Introduction

Question: Which book gives the best definition of family, the dictionary or the Bible? (Hint: Don't even reach for the dictionary.)

If ever there were a clear distinction between the secular and the spiritual, it's right here on my desk. Two books. One inspired with truth that touches the heart and meets us right where we live, the other totally out of touch with the heart of the matter.

In describing family, the dictionary fails to mention love, support, or training. It doesn't talk about burps or midnight feedings. Nothing about Little League games or the comfort of Mom's bed in a thunderstorm. Instead of defining, it dissects, and then leaves out the best part.

I have other things on my desk that speak about family. Lots of photos, for instance. In the blink of an eye, faster

IT TAKES
a
FAMILY

than a computer cursor can zero in on an icon, these photos draw data from my memory bank that tells me not only what a family is, but also who I am. But I know, of course, that in spite of pretty poses and scenic settings, life isn't always picture-perfect. We want to forget sad scenes and tough times as quickly as possible. But not the lessons they teach. Yes, life is full of mystery. That's why families are essential.

The very first "church" that God formed was the family. What better way to worship together? If one member hurts, we all hurt; if one member exults, we all applaud. If one member of the family is missing for whatever reason, God isn't. God wants to be our constant Comforter, and the focus of our celebrations.

This book celebrates family. Together let's explore its importance and how to repair it when it needs mending.

The Sugarplum Tree

IT TAKES *a* FAMILY

My wife and I raised our two children on twenty-eight acres of beautiful trees, moss, fiddlehead ferns, and rippling brooks. An amazing outdoor classroom to study with awe the wonders of God's creation!

Damming up the brooks to make ponds became an excuse for many exciting projects. Some dams required bulldozers, others a few bags of cement, and for still others, we simply piled up stones. The study of salamanders and crawfish was an engrossing offshoot of one such project. To build nature trails I bought a used Jeep, complete with snowplow and large circular saw, for $350. We were really into those woods.

The biggest attraction for our children was a large maple tree we called the sugarplum tree. Before we bought the property a woodpecker had hammered out a convenient hole in the tree, slightly higher than the eye level of our young children.

We would sit under its cool branches and talk and tell stories. And then came the best part. Our children would say the "magic" words and I'd lift them up to the old woodpecker hole. Lo and behold,

there were goodies inside! A few candies. Maybe a couple of cookies. The contents didn't matter that much. This was a moment of priceless wonder.

(Harry Winston, eat your heart out: A gumdrop is often more valuable than a five-carat diamond.)

I'm so thankful that God gave us those acres and those years. But I'm also thankful that inside the mind of every child— no matter where they grow up—is imagination just waiting to be tapped. No matter where God puts us, we can take hold of our children and lift them up to see the enchantment and adventure of life.

Family Thank Tank

1. What could be your family's sugarplum tree?

_____

_____

_____

_____

_____

2. How can you share the evidence of God's creation with your family?

_____

_____

_____

_____

_____

Genes

IT TAKES *a* FAMILY

You're wearing my jeans!

What household hasn't reverberated when a sibling sounds that siren? But try this one on for size.

You're wearing my genes!

> **Genes.** An element of sperm plasm that carries hereditary characteristics that form a specific part of a self-perpetuating chromosome in the cell nucleus.

Whew! You don't have to be a biological technocrat to know that genes are big today. They're being isolated, split, altered, withdrawn, and injected as never before.

Do we need a megamillion-dollar microscope to spot a gene? Does it take special training?

Nope!

She's got her mother's eyes. There! Someone spotted her mother's genes in that girl. He's got his father's chin. There ya go again. The father's genes are alive and well.

IT TAKES
a
FAMILY

Look around. There are genes for the color of hair, eyes, and skin. Genes for our bones, muscles, arteries, nerves—every single amazing part of us, inside and out.

Would you like to read the greatest book ever written on genealogy? Well, you can not only read the book, you can meet the Author and, by the way, He's also the Creator.

In the very first chapter of His Book, the Bible, God explains that every living thing—man, woman, plant, and animal—will have a seed that will always distinguish its character. God says elsewhere that He doesn't look at the outside—the physical results of our genes—the way we do. He looks at the inside. The heart of the matter is that He's telling us what's important in life. God's talking about the spirit He breathed into us. Our souls.

Long after our bodies have creaked and sagged for the last time, that unseen power, that dimension of life within us all, lives on by the grace of the Author of our faith.

Are you getting goosebumps yet?

Yes, it's important to take care of our bodies. Exercise. Diet. Cut your hair

IT TAKES *a* FAMILY

once in a while. Our genetic appearance says something about us, but it doesn't necessarily tell the truth. We can X-ray and MRI almost every part of our bodies, but can we measure that part of us that only God can see? There is so much in us and around us that's visible only to Him.

The Bible defines wisdom as seeing things as God sees them. No mortal can hope to attain that kind of vision. Would contact lenses help? Well, the more we're in contact with Him, the better we'll see things. The better we'll see ourselves. And with the Omnipotent Optometrist sharpening our focus, maybe we'll see things that don't normally meet the eye. Things that are shrouded in mystery, wrapped in wonder, and written between the lines. Things that transcend time and generations. We're rubbing shoulders now with the divine.

Yes, our genes are God's gift to us and all our progeny. High-tech tinkering, for all its wizardry, will never change the dynamic that God created in each one. But we're talking about reproducing ourselves spiritually. Only God can do that, and He's made us part of that miracle.

IT TAKES
a
FAMILY

Jesus spoke earnestly to Nicodemus one night. The religious leader had come to Jesus to learn the source of His remarkable power. Jesus gave the answer to Nicodemus and to all who seek eternal truth: Men can only reproduce human life, but the Holy Spirit gives new life from heaven. Just as Moses in the wilderness lifted up a bronze image of a serpent on a pole, so also was Jesus lifted up on a cross. For God so loved the world that He gave His only Son so that anyone who believes in Him shall not perish, but have eternal life.

Jesus came and died for us. Because of His sacrifice, our sins have been forgiven. But that's not all. Three days later Jesus rose from the grave. Alive. Victory over death was His, and is ours the minute we truly know Him in a personal way.

We have so much more to leave as an inheritance than the color of our eyes or hair. Yes, we give life to our children. We care for them and train them and pray for them. But above all, we need to be sure they know the One who is truly above all. That's the greatest living trust we can create. All who follow us will be the beneficiaries.

Family Thank Tank

1. How many of God's spiritual wonders can you count?

_____

_____

_____

_____

_____

2. Would you like to number more? (Ask Him to help you count better.)

_____

_____

_____

_____

_____

The Family
Album

IT TAKES *a* FAMILY

When we build a house, we add paint and paper to the walls. When we build a home, we use family photos.

When we move, we don't take the paint and paper with us, but the family photos are never left behind. The pictures go with us because they're part of us.

My wife smiles at me from every corner of my studio. Her pictures are everywhere.

Her engagement photo when she looked like an All-American prom queen. A va-va-va-voom picture she sent overseas when I was an Air Force pilot during World War II. That photo did more to get me through my missions than all the briefing sessions I attended.

But today, outside the photo-lined walls of our family home, we know it's a different world. Despite how much love and training we pour into our children's lives, there are rampant social viruses at work—at school, on the ballfield, at the mall—ready to invade our dear ones.

We really get on our knees when our children choose a mate. There's excitement in "getting married." There's also responsibility and commitment in "being

IT TAKES
a
FAMILY

married." So as we pass by our extended family album, we're so thankful that our children are married to children whose parents gave them love and values that prepared them for a fruitful marriage. These times need authentic, compassionate, and loving Christian testimony.

Our photo gallery flows through many rooms, but it also travels with us. As grandparents, my wife and I come with a full set of photos of our grandchildren. "Show and tell" begins anytime, anywhere we have an audience.

Why is it that grandchildren never carry pictures of their grandparents? The answer is found in God's gravity. Love flows down. That's the way it is. God pours His love through one generation after the other. That's not to say that grandchildren don't love their grandparents. Of course they do, but God gives each generation a special kind of love that perfectly fits each member of the family.

God builds families with the facets of a fine diamond. But diamonds can be bought for a price. God's family is priceless.

So we honor and respect our

IT TAKES
a
FAMILY

differences. We are all individuals and, as Jesus said, they shall know us by our love. Our family photos surround us with the joy of sharing that love.

Family Thank Tank

1. In your family album who has the biggest smile?

_____

_____

_____

_____

_____

2. Can you see Jesus reflected in any of the pictures?

_____

_____

_____

_____

_____

Roots
and Wings

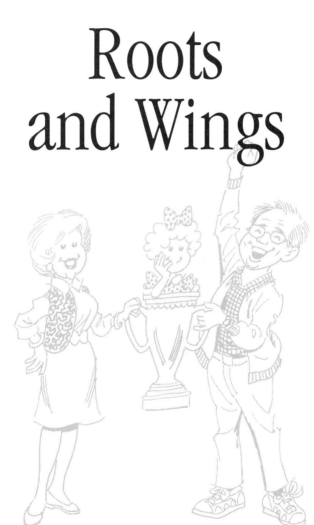

IT TAKES *a* FAMILY

Noah was the first grandparent to build a lifeboat out of the family tree. God called it an ark. God is still using arks—*patri-arks* and *matri-arks*—because the world hasn't changed that much. It's still deluged with all kinds of threatening storms that can erode and engulf our families.

Psalm 127 speaks of children as arrows, and happy is the man who has a quiver full of them. Happier still is the man who points each arrow in the same direction...straight to God.

But in these days when both parents must work to make ends meet, the children end up at loose ends. A latch key isn't exactly a master key to the heart. Latch keys often open the door to loneliness and the kind of vacuum that is filled by negative electronic influences that enter our homes at the flick of a remote control. In some cases one or both parents may no longer be part of the family.

When parents are not present, for whatever reason, the grandparents often become at least part-time foster parents. And full-time is not out of the realm of possibility.

IT TAKES
a
FAMILY

Needless to say, this seems at first glance to create a "generation gap" that no teen of the 60s and 70s could have conjured. One minute Gramps and Grandma are in their Lazy Boys, the next they're on a trampoline. Make that a rocket launch that's lifted them to a moonscape of truly weightless values! Welcome to outer space.

We've all seen enough pictures from outer space to know that the view is breathtaking from up there. When grandparents revert to the role of parents, that can take your breath away, too. Put simply, though, everyone is hurting. Grandparents are out of their comfort zones. Parents, for a variety of tragic reasons, are unable to give their children what they need most. And the children are in the worst position of all. Confused, perhaps bitter, and hurt, they are inclined to fill the emptiness of their lives with the first attractive option they can find.

And now the good news. With God's help...

Noah never built an ark before, but he did it.

He never rode the world's first

IT TAKES a FAMILY

round-up before, but he did it.

He never saw such a storm before, but he got through it.

And behold, Noah never saw such a rainbow before! God sent it.

> "As long as the earth endures, seedtime and harvest, cold and heat, summer and winter, day and night will never cease."
>
> Genesis 8:22

If God fulfills a promise of that enormity, we can trust Him for every circumstance of our lives. The tides of this world come and go. And God parts water when He has to.

Grandparents and grandchildren have a special relationship that God wants to nurture, and He will. Let love flow, for blossoming branches need strong, sturdy roots. Probably the most pithy advice ever coined for the older generation is this: "We need to give our children two things—roots and wings."

Before those roots can go down, though, a lot of spade work may be required, and not necessarily in the

IT TAKES
a
FAMILY

garden. This can involve ball fields, fishing poles, model building, homework assignments, cookie baking—all kinds of activities that bring you together in ways that quickly bridge the age difference. In fact, the years aren't really an obstacle. They can be a real blessing—for both of you. And remember, young people don't rebel against authority. They rebel against the lack of it.

None of us today is called on to build an ark, but we're all called to save our family. No matter where that call leads us, we can be sure God will be there to bless us, and our family.

Family Thank Tank

1. How close do you feel to your grandchildren/grand-parents?

_____

_____

_____

_____

_____

2. How long has it been since you sent them a letter? Told them you love them?

_____

_____

_____

_____

_____

Priorities

IT TAKES
a
FAMILY

There's no way we can approach God intellectually. But rest assured, He's not an ivory tower kind of God. He wants to be right with us in all the nitty-gritty of life, not far off in space, keeping the stars in order.

Scripture tells us that just as the heavens are higher than the earth, God's ways are higher than our ways. How can we make the "Highway" our way?

To begin, love for our family is our first priority, right? Wrong! I remember the world-class wrestling match I had with this one.

I confidently assumed that God would be smiling broadly and cheering me on, the more I loved my family. I was certain the best thing I could do for my children was to love their mother. I was sure God would say "Amen" to those sentiments.

But, let's face it, I'm limited by my human nature. I will always fall short because of secular booby traps. To paraphrase the apostle Paul in the seventh chapter of Romans, I can't do what I want to do, and yet I do what I don't want to do.

Transporting this Scripture right through my front door, I find that there are times when I lose my cool. I get out of bed

IT TAKES
a
FAMILY

with the very best intentions. I love my family. I want to be the world's best husband and father. Why don't I measure up?

Life is not a do-it-yourself project. Our toolbox isn't adequate. We need to bring in the heavy equipment. God says love Me first. Make Him Number One.

Love Him more than my wife? My kids? Yes. More than anything else.

Hmmm. That sounds like tough theology. Even if I accept the doctrine, how do I practice it? I mean, it seems like I'm taking something away from my family. Is that what God wants?

No. God never wants to take away good things. He wants to give us more! Put another way, no matter how hard we try, we'll never have harmony in our families if God is playing "second fiddle." It all comes down to this. When God is the head of the house, everyone is looking in the same direction. In short, everything will start looking up.

When I put God first, He helps me with all my other priorities. He enables me to love my wife more. He brings a greater quality of love and life into the whole family. And it's not just love that's enriched. Every

IT TAKES
a
FAMILY

family today is faced with situations that call for the patience of Job and the wisdom of Solomon. Guess what? Where do you suppose they got those virtues?

Our family councils today need a counselor who's "out of this world," as the kids would say, but "down to earth," as we would put it. We all need a Spirit in our homes that establishes our attitudes and controls our behavior.

Paul defined our problem in Romans 7:24-25.

> "What a wretched man I am! Who will rescue me from this body of death? Thanks be to God—through Jesus Christ our Lord!"

Take God at His Word. God's Son Jesus Christ paid the price for our sins on the cross of Calvary. Now if we accept Jesus to be God's Son, we can also accept freely His incomparable love. God wants your life to overflow with His love; He knows every family has room for more. Every family should know the joy of living each day for God, the joy of sharing God's love. Every family should make God their top priority.

Family Thank Tank

1. Read 1 Corinthians 13, verses 4 through 7. What can you do to share this kind of love in your family?

_____

_____

_____

_____

_____

2. Do you thank God for His pure love?

_____

_____

_____

_____

_____

Train Up a Child

IT TAKES
a
FAMILY

Extension course 101 on this subject is conducted daily at your local supermarket. Listen to this exhausted mother:

"Danny, I said don't roll the melons down the aisle!"

"Danny, please don't squirt detergent on everyone!"

"Danny, be careful...you're knocking that...oh, Danny [gasp]...." Crash!

Is Danny paying attention? Is he obeying or is he having a good time?

Actually, he's having a ball. Neither he nor his mother has heard of the "positive no." The magic word that tells the child the parent means what she says. A word that is backed by the full power and integrity of the governing body. It does not need repeating. It's good for the parent's state of mind and the child's state of behind. It completely eliminates the pitiful progression of pleading that produces petrified parents.

"Please! I'm warning you! I'm telling you for the last time! Once more and you'll be sorry! Did you hear me?"

The more the threats come, the weaker they get. And the stronger anarchy sets in. The child has learned that empty words

carry no weight.

Sure, if we apply sufficient pressure and increase it as many notches as necessary, we will eventually push our children to do something. The problem with this losing kind of motivational game is demonstrated in our supermarket example. Neither the child nor the parent is taking the matter seriously. They're playing games, and all the shoppers know who's winning.

Time out! How about a better game plan? Instead of teaching a child to *do* something, let's teach him to *be* something. Be obedient. Be respectful. Be attitude. Be long. Be love.

Okay. Sounds great. Uh, how do we start?

In reverse order. If a child truly feels loved and that love is always on display, he or she will develop a strong self-worth in a very positive sense. Without that assurance of love, a child feels they're not worth much. A child can be like a computer. What we put in comes out.

It's evident even in the cradle that a child doesn't have to be taught to be bad. But they have to be taught to be good. If

IT TAKES a FAMILY

a parent doesn't teach, a child will tend to go as far as he or she can—in the wrong direction.

Obedience comes from respect, and respect is caught much easier than it's taught. All the emotions and qualities of human nature are contagious. We need to guarantee our homes against all the negatives and saturate them with the positives.

The worst virus to spread in our homes is neglect. Satan will surely fill that void with every trick from every aisle of his well-stocked supermarket.

No matter how large or how small the family, a child needs to know he belongs. That he's an important part. That there's love to receive and love to give. And sharing that love is what families are all about.

Family Thank Tank

1. Which do you throw the most, kisses or insults?

_____

_____

_____

_____

_____

2. Do you sing together in your home? (Try harmony and be sure to sing your part.)

_____

_____

_____

_____

_____

Cradles and Cocoons

IT TAKES
a
FAMILY

The young parents stood beside the crib of their firstborn. Awe. Silence. Eyes transfixed. They seemed focused on a miracle.

Finally, the enraptured young wife punctured the sanctuary of their thoughts. "What are you thinking, honey?"

His answer overpowered her demure, sweet voice. "For the life of me, I can't see how they can build that crib for eighty-nine bucks."

Not exactly a Kodak moment!

Thankfully, not typical. Other young parents also stand in amazement beside their cribs. But they see far more than a price tag. They see bone of their bones and flesh of their flesh. They know God has blessed them with the privilege of participating in the wonder of His creation.

These parents know the speed of the times. Two months on a shelf and a computer is obsolete. Today's paycheck may be tomorrow's dismissal notice.

They look inside that crib with more reverence than ever. Outside things are disposable. Inside—inside the crib—things are eternal. God has His arms around that baby, the parents are certain. They've read the Bible. They've dedicated

IT TAKES
a
FAMILY

their child to God.

It's impossible to keep young people still. It's especially hard to corral their thoughts at a time like this. They're looking into the future. They'll teach the child to walk, talk, ride a bike, take the school bus, drive a car.

Seventeen years run through their reverie. If they're really forward thinkers, they have the child off to college in the next breath. And then [gasp] the child has really flown the coop and marries and starts a family.

Let's back up a minute. Ask any grandparent, how fast did the years pass between then and now? All of a sudden life is on fast forward. Many would like to stop and have a replay.

Actually, the button has always been on replay. That's what children and grandchildren do for us. They give us the chance to relive life from a different perspective. Actually, the credit should go to God. He—and He alone—makes it possible for us to enjoy the indescribable role of grandparenting. Our energy levels and other vital signs are lagging, but who makes a better baby sitter or holiday host

IT TAKES *a* FAMILY

than Grandma and Grandpa?

The old get older, and their genes come in beautiful new packages. Life cycles evolve and revolve as God unwinds the silver cord around His fingers. That cord holds families and generations together because its sacred spindle makes such a tight weave.

We sing "Blest be the tie that binds" and refer to the family of God. Within that family God cements the human family with a sense of oneness that clings better than any glue.

Where are you on God's silver cord? A young baby is too young to know it exists, but it only takes a few months to know how to hold on and pull yourself along. The cord has a secure, comfortable feel during the early years.

Then comes the time when we're tempted to let go, to find a different cord. Some might even tie knots in the cord or make the kind of mess that seems impossible to untangle. And, from a human standpoint, some knots we tie are so impossible they make the Gordian knot seem like child's play.

Are you crying 911 because you're at

IT TAKES
a
FAMILY

the end of your rope? Dangling, entangled, helpless? Maybe you're footloose and fancy free but a loved one is bound by some noose you can't untie.

Whatever metaphor fits the situation, God will provide the metamorphosis. We all know how a caterpillar spins a cocoon, sleeps a while, and then ultimately breaks free of that self-made chamber, not as a lowly worm but a butterfly, with a brand-new life ahead.

God's silver cord is in that cocoon, and in the ones spun by hapless humans. Its end, in fact, is hanging out, ready for God's tug to set us free.

Don't ever let go of that silver cord. No matter how high the wall between you and a loved one, no matter how wide the chasm, hold on and pray. God doesn't divide; He multiplies.

Family Thank Tank

1. What kind of cocoon do you know? (A secret place, a quiet room, a shopping mall, within yourself?)

_____

_____

_____

_____

_____

2. Have you asked God to release you from your cocoon and bring you into the light?

_____

_____

_____

_____

Take Your Temperament

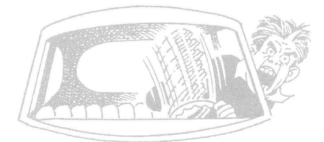

IT TAKES *a* FAMILY

There are four basic personality types: choleric, phlegmatic, sanguine, and melancholy. Every family has an assortment of these temperaments. Often some folks fit more than one category, but the nature of the various characteristics is consistently a part of who we are.

After the four temperaments are explained, see if you can identify each family member. Try your friends. Remember, one category is neither better nor worse than the other. They're just different because God made us all special and unique. Have fun!

Phlegmatic Fred. The natural-born couch potato, Fred has elevated his favorite habit to an art form with the advent of the remote control. It's an art form that definitely falls under the still-life category!

He's an introvert, a pessimist, and a watcher—there's the couch potato again. Inclined to be shy and reticent, he's definitely not the life-of-the-party type.

On the plus side, he's calm, cool, and collected. He keeps his emotions hidden. Never in a hurry. Good under pressure. Resents being pushed. (No, we're not

talking about your refrigerator here.) Fred is easy to get along with, a good listener.

Since he's never in a hurry, he has time for the children. He's sympathetic and kind, living a patient, easy-going life.

He's really an all-purpose person.

Sanguine Sally. Hold on to your hats! Here she comes! A compulsive talker and story-teller, she holds on to her audience as she bubbles animatedly. Sally's loaded with energy and enthusiasm. She loves people. She's never met a stranger, but better, she prevents dull moments and creates sponta-neous activities. Two sanguines in the same room would drive each other crazy.

Sanguine Sally answers before she hears the full question. She thinks out loud as she touches, grabs, squeezes, and pummels the person sitting next to her. She constantly campaigns for Miss Congeniality. Her home is carnival time from sun-up to sundown. Then she really comes alive.

She's creative, colorful, and a great friend.

Melancholy Millie. Poor Millie gets a bum

rap with that melancholy moniker. She isn't as sad and depressed as it sounds. In fact, she's very talented and creative, deep and thoughtful. Very orderly in her home. In fact, when her husband gets out of bed during the night, she's liable to make the bed by the time he gets back.

She's deeply concerned for other people's welfare and will sacrifice her own will for others. This type of temperament is extremely analytical and resourceful but will often set unrealistic goals. They can be hypochondria-prone.

In terms of affection, Millie is just the opposite of Sally. She avoids calling attention to herself. She's content to stay in the background and is a very faithful and loyal friend.

Choleric Charlie. Charlie is a "type A" personality who burns the candle at both ends and asks the Lord for more wax.

He's a workaholic. However, when you have your nose to the grindstone, your shoulder to the wheel, and your eye on the ball, it's hard to keep track of your family. He tends to make decisions quickly and is impatient with poor performance. Even

though he's strong-willed and comes on strong, he's a born leader.

He's not easily discouraged; he doesn't get ulcers, but he gives them to others. He seems to thrive on controversy and arguments and excels in emergencies. Charlie has little need for friends and is inclined to dominate the ones he has. When driving he has a lead foot. But when the chips are down, Charlie's your man. He exudes confidence and can run anything.

Each temperament has its strengths and weaknesses. Once we get a good look in the mirror, we want to take hold of those wise words Johnny Mercer wrote: "Accentuate the positive, eliminate the negative, don't mess with Mr. In-Between."

While we're recognizing our differences, we want to remember that we don't all get out on the same side of the bed each day. We want to allow room for our family and friends to have off days. The day we feel on top of the world may be the same day someone else's chin is bouncing on their knees. Support them. Encourage them. But allow them to work through

IT TAKES *a* FAMILY

the dark cloud that envelops them. Trust that your sunshine will brighten their day. Don't give them sunburn.

In his first letter to the Corinthians, Paul writes of the body of Christ—the church—in a way that could apply to families today. Paul explains that just as there are many parts of our bodies, so it is with Christ's body. We are all part of the church. When one part hurts, we all hurt. It takes all of us to make the body complete. We belong to each other and we need each other.

Accept each other as Christ accepts us—just as we are.

Family Thank Tank

1. Did you identify your temperament type?

_____

_____

_____

_____

_____

2. Do you know the joy of giving your God-given talents back to God so He can use them?

_____

_____

_____

_____

_____

Aquatic
Lesson

IT TAKES
a
FAMILY

Porpoises are well known as the playthings of the ocean. Boaters constantly thrill to their antics in their wakes and by their bows. Scientists study their radarlike "ping" sounds to learn their secrets of communication and to improve naval submarine detection.

Whether in water, classroom, or laboratory, porpoises can teach us a great deal about getting along together.

Once my friend was boating and entered Tarpon Bay, a large body of water that cuts into the back of Sanibel Island in Florida. He followed a slick of red that he quickly determined was blood. Then he came to the source of the blood—a porpoise giving birth. Surrounding the mother porpoise were about a dozen other porpoises forming a ring of protection.

What happened then is almost unbelievable. At the moment of birth two porpoises from the protective ring dove down and lifted the newborn to the surface for its first breath of air.

The boaters beheld it all in total silence, afraid any sound would interrupt the sanctity and tenderness of such a moment. They had observed the great

IT TAKES *a* FAMILY

miracle of life taking place. And they had seen a family at work in the ongoing process of protecting, supporting, and encouraging. Helping one another. Being a family.

There was a baby and a mother. I'm sure the proud father was there, too. I have no idea if porpoises have aunts and uncles; surely they have grandparents. In any event, that group of porpoises leap-frogged all the scientists measuring sonic signals and sent us a message that goes straight to the heart. When there's a need, swim straight to the rescue.

The applications for this story hardly end. How many family members come to mind who could use a strong ring around them? Do you know a mother who needs a circle of friends? Are there any young ones who don't need a lift?

Are your small groups at church doing as well as the porpoises?

The porpoise certainly knows how to communicate. That's an essential art for any family, small, large, or extended.

And finally, when we get the message that a need exists, are we ready to drop everything and answer the call?

Family Thank Tank

1. How do you think it felt to be part of a group like the protective ring?

_____

_____

_____

_____

_____

2. What do you think would have happened if a shark had tried to join the circle?

_____

_____

_____

_____

God Gives
Family to the
Lonely

IT TAKES
a
FAMILY

Not all of us are blessed with a tight circle of loving family and friends. Some of us may be in more like a cyclone. We seem to be going round and round, but getting nowhere. A storm is raging and we have no one to talk to. No one to reach out to. No shoulder to cry on. No hope.

It's the worst spot in the world. But hear this and take comfort: Many of us have been there. We've felt the same loneliness and fear. And many of us have found the way out. We remember the frustrations that fill that pit like a quagmire of quicksand. The harder we struggle, the deeper we seem to sink.

And now the good news. It's too good not to share.

Read Psalm 40:2,3:

"He lifted me out of the slimy pit, out of the mud and mire; he set my feet on a rock and gave me a firm place to stand. He put a new song in my mouth, a hymn of praise to our God."

Are you in the pit right now? Would you like to feel God's strong hand? Reach

out. Take it!

But wait, you say, the mess you're in is absolutely impossible. Really?

God sees it differently. Jesus said,

"What is impossible with men is possible with God."

Luke 18:27

With God, all things are possible!

He doesn't just bring relief. He doesn't just give you a second wind. He'll fill your life with such a spirit of enthusiastic joy you'll find yourself singing that new song with gusto. He gives you Himself. God has a very special set of lyrics, just for you.

God doesn't perform cookie-cutter miracles. Each one of his children is unique, with their own individual problems and needs.

Truly, God's creation is beyond our comprehension. The Hubbel telescope is only beginning to give us a glimpse of the enormity of the universe. Electronic microscopes have only started to pierce the secrets inside life's tiniest particles. Yet, in a world of billions, God knows your name and He knows your situation. Better still,

IT TAKES *a* FAMILY

He knows the answer to the greatest need of your life.

The true wonder is not just in experiencing God lift you out of the pit. The real excitement is in seeing how He does it. Watch God at work: He does things no one ever thought of doing. He pulls things out of left field. He has legions of angels you've never met before.

God has got something special for you. Recognize Him as your Father. He'll give you a family to love you.

Family Thank Tank

1. Have you really prayed to God lately?

_____

_____

_____

_____

_____

2. Are you open to receive His answers, and His peace?

_____

_____

_____

_____

_____

Hand-Me-Downs or Handcuffs?

IT TAKES
a
FAMILY

As a cartoonist and writer, I've worked at home throughout my career. My studio was part of the house. No commuting. No wasted time going or coming. No travel expenses. Just a short walk from the breakfast room to my studio. Then a short walk back for lunch. Ditto for supper.

I can hear the chorus of female readers now: "His poor wife!"

Yes, she had me around all day long, day after day after day! Some readers might find it hard to believe that a marriage could survive such an arrangement for so long.

From my standpoint it was a dream situation. I loved my work—drawing Archie, Jughead, Betty, and Veronica, and a family of comic figures whose sole role was to tickle the funny bone—and I loved my wife. However, I was so engrossed in my work that I typically was holed up in my studio, out of Hermine's way.

Hermine did the usual entertaining and neither her activity nor mine bothered the other. In fact, when she was out, I was able to take her phone calls. It never occurred to me (until now) that I was the world's first answering machine.

IT TAKES
a
FAMILY

By far the greatest blessing from working at home was the togetherness we had as a family. I saw my children grow up. I was with them for every meal. We had ball games on the lawn every afternoon and ping-pong in the basement at night. When winter came we built award-winning snowmen and skated on the lake in our backyard. I'd simply work all night at the drawing board to make up for any lost time.

Today as a grandparent I see the same pattern in the home of my son, who is a pastor. In spite of an extremely demanding schedule, he and his wife make time for their four children, and the results are immediately visible. Each of their bedrooms looks like a trophy display store, the rewards of playing the game with enthusiasm and doing the best you can.

Life gives all kinds of verdicts and awards. Some to be desired, some to be avoided.

Bill Glass had an expanding trophy case as he grew up in Texas. In college he won All-American honors on the gridiron, and later became All-Pro in professional football. Then he took on the greatest scrimmage of his life. He became an evangelist whose goal was to touch the lives of prisoners with the kind of freedom that only Christ can bring.

Today the Bill Glass Evangelistic Association goes inside prisons week after week, with as many as 1400 lay counselors, to deal one on one with inmates who have just heard the Gospel of Jesus Christ. Each lay counselor pays his own way for these prison crusades, spending two or three days inside the prison.

The fruit of Bill's ministry and others, such as Chuck Colson, proves that only by the power of God will America ever come to grips with its escalating crime epidemic. Every other effort has been a dismal failure. Bill's success reminds us that the best time to fix a problem is before it grows up. And he has a message, not only for inmates, but for every father in America.

Recently Bill spoke to forty-four prisoners on death row in Parchment, Mississippi. He asked each one how they got along with their dads. All of them answered, "I hated him." Bill has had that answer confirmed in every prison he's

IT TAKES
a
FAMILY

entered. Prisoners consistently reflect a broken relationship with their fathers.

Here's another amazing statistic: The Jewish population in prisons is virtually zero. Jewish families traditionally have a strong sense of heritage. It's customary for the father to bestow "the blessing" on his son. More than a ritual, this gesture tells the son he is loved, that he belongs to a unit that will do anything for him and expects the same from him in return.

In Cook County Juvenile Center in Chicago, Bill asked nine to twelve year olds these questions: Are you in a gang? Do you carry a gun? Do you use drugs? Are you active sexually?

Every single one answered yes to every single question.

Then Bill asked the clincher: How many of you have a father who lives at home? Not one of those children could answer yes.

Here is another alarming discovery Bill made in prisons everywhere. The older prisoners are literally scared to death of the young inmates. Bill found that the young prisoners have absolutely no conscience. No fear. Their impulses have no limits. A

IT TAKES a FAMILY

cell will contain them for a time but most of them will eventually be released to repeat their crimes over and over again. In their eyes, the mistake is not in what they do, but in getting caught. Society beware. They intend to do better the next time.

Walls will never be high enough or strong enough to contain the rage that grows without a parent's love and involvement. We start out playing games with our children, but the stakes get higher as they grow. The worst discovery any parent can make is to climb the ladder of success, reach the top, and then find they've climbed the wrong ladder. What matters most has been left behind.

"Hand-me-downs" used to be a less than appealing expression, but handing down love, involvement, and training to succeeding generations is surely the best way to ensure they will indeed be succeeding generations.

Family Thank Tank

1. Have you told your parents and children how much you love them?

_____

_____

_____

_____

_____

2. Have you thanked God today for all your blessings?

_____

_____

_____

_____

_____

The Family
Bible

IT TAKES *a* FAMILY

Immediately below *family* in the dictionary is the listing *family Bible* with this definition: "A large Bible having special pages to record births, marriages, and deaths."

Let me tell you about my wife's family Bible. It's almost as large as our TV set, with more information than the Discovery Channel.

Her Bible was printed in Europe centuries ago and came to America in steerage during the 1890s. To preserve such an heirloom, we had a museumlike plexiglass case made just for that Bible.

What makes this family Bible so special are the notes and testimonies it contains. Each was written by people of faith who lived as the Bible told them to live. They prayed for each other. But that's not all. These folks, centuries ago, prayed for us, today. How's that for a definition of family? Members praying for succeeding generations hundreds of years in the future.

Have you ever driven along the interstate and thanked the Lord for those who paved the way? It's only natural to go on our merry way and simply take the smooth

IT TAKES
a
FAMILY

road for granted. We have no idea whether the foreman showed up for work with a splitting headache or a bad back. All we know is that the road is open.

Like our highways, our heritage had a beginning. My wife's family Bible taught us how much of our path has been paved with prayer, from a long time ago.

Most of us know the story of the Philippian jailer. When the Lord sent an earthquake to release Paul and Silas from prison, the jailer was sure the Romans would hold him responsible. He said to the two Christians, "What must I do to be saved?"

Paul and Silas's answer is found in Acts 16:31:

"Believe in the Lord Jesus, and you will be saved—you and your household."

In other words, God is telling us that when we accept Christ as Lord of our lives, not only will we have constant fellowship with Him, but that blessing will extend to every member of our family.

My wife and I claimed that special

IT TAKES
a
FAMILY

promise of God when we became Christians thirty years ago. Oh, we considered ourselves Christians before that, but we were Christians by process of elimination. After all, we weren't members of other world faiths. Therefore, we were Christians. We believed God was somewhere out there. Christ died for us, but that was a long time ago.

Our prayers were really spiritual shopping lists. We had no assurance that our prayers would be answered. We didn't even know if they were being heard. Nevertheless, because of God's promise and our faithful prayers, over thirty of our family found there was far more to Christianity than we ever imagined.

Until we get to heaven, none of us will ever know all the prayers that have been said on our behalf. No matter how big our pinheads, we'll never be able to count the number of "angels unaware" who have been our invisible rescue squads time and time again. That's a spiritual reality that should be of tremendous encouragement to us, especially when we're tempted to feel all alone.

Here's a first-hand example of the

IT TAKES
a
FAMILY

power of prayer. My wife's sister Fran was included every day in our prayers. Since Fran resisted our attempts to share our faith, we felt that perhaps God had someone else in mind to be His witness. However, Fran lived hundreds of miles from us and, as new Christians, our circle of Christian friends didn't extend that far.

My wife had just started a Christian Women's Club on Sanibel Island, Florida, and was familiar with their nationwide organization. She wrote their headquarters and asked if they would have a member in Fran's area make contact and share the Gospel with her.

The result was that Doris Durham of Chattanooga, Tennessee, drove fifty miles to Fran's home in Georgia, not knowing if anyone was home, with no preparation other than considerable prayer and the assurance that when we go anywhere in the Lord's name, He prepares the way. Doris's clock was set on God's perfect time. Oh, what a welcome He arranged.

Doris rang Fran's doorbell. God opened the door. Fran wasn't expecting anyone, especially an evangelistic Christian, but she was ready. Her heart was heavy and she needed to unburden herself. Fran and Doris had a heartfelt conversation. Then they talked to God. Two women who started out as strangers ended up as sisters. God had a new child.

My phone rang later that day. It was Fran with a brand-new tone in her voice. "Al," she said, "I've just received Jesus as my Savior!"

Another entry in our family Bible. Another example of how our God, to whom nothing is impossible, turns the most difficult things inside out.

For all the happy endings in life, we still face riddles none of us can solve. More than just question marks, we encounter tough nuts we can't crack. That's when we go to our family Bible. God, who created life, knows how we can deal with it successfully. And He's given us a family to share the adventure.

Family Thank Tank

1. How many family members do you pray for?

_____

_____

_____

_____

_____

2. How many do you suppose pray for you?

_____

_____

_____

_____

_____

Archie's
Family

IT TAKES *a* FAMILY

As the writer and artist of Archie Comics and Archie Christian Comics, I'm often asked how I create the stories and visual excitement, day after day.

The answer is easy. I've got a lot of Archie in me. Archie really doesn't intend to mess up. Neither do I.

When I draw Archie panicking as he enters the school principal's office, I can draw it convincingly because I remember what it was like. When Archie doesn't get the girl he'd like for a date, I remember that feeling, too.

Archie is really Everyman. Everyone can identify with Archie because only one person in all history did things perfectly. The rest of us mess up from time to time. (Archie is a case in point: He's been in high school for fifty-five years and no one expects him to graduate!)

The big appeal to those who pick up an Archie comic is that they know him and all the other characters so well. Like a member of the family, the reader knows how each character will behave. If I tinkered with any of the characters and changed their personalities, the comic would suffer.

IT TAKES *a* FAMILY

We know what that can be like in our own families, don't we? If a member acts strangely, or not like themselves, we feel immediate concern. When the pattern persists, it can reach crisis proportions.

Personality is a unique quality. Whether pleasant or unpleasant, people know us by our personalities. When someone hands us a rose, are we impressed by the fragrance or the thorns? It depends how they give it to us.

So, as I draw a slice of life each day, I try to sketch folks we recognize and are comfortable with—and above all have fun with.

Unlike Archie, Jughead isn't interested in girls. He loves food. Any kind of food. Reggie is a great athlete, and he knows it. His ego demands that he never let his friends forget it. Betty is an all-American girl with a heart of gold. She wears it on her sleeve for Archie, but he's more interested in...Veronica! She's a spoiled rich girl who only dates Archie as a last resort.

Big Ethel could be mistaken for a comic valentine. She's not very attractive, but, interestingly, she has received more fan mail than any of the others. I created

IT TAKES a FAMILY

Big Ethel as a model millions of readers could identify with. She's not asked out on dates. She has a poor self-image and is prone to pity parties, hence all the letters from readers in the same boat.

"Big Ethel, I know how you feel. My friends make fun of me, too."

"Big Ethel, sometimes it's so bad I don't want to go to school."

My purpose with Big Ethel, however, was to offer more than empathy. She offers victory and success over the heartache of low self-esteem and loneliness.

A typical story might show her looking in the mirror and lamenting, "If this is an example of God's creation, forget it!" In other words, "How can I have faith in a God who would do this to me?" Immediately, countless readers connect with Big Ethel. Their nose is too big. Their eyes are too small. They didn't get the right chin.

In her anguish, Big Ethel picks up the Bible and learns that God doesn't look on the outside as people do; God looks at the heart. God doesn't just love beauty queens. He loves everyone He made—just

IT TAKES a FAMILY

as they are. She learns that true beauty isn't really found in the flesh. It's found in the spirit.

And then Big Ethel makes a life-changing discovery. God gives each of us special gifts, a special talent. With His help, we can find that gift, allow God to bless it, and help us to use it in a way that makes us a blessing to others. Then folks will see us not for how we look, but for what we are.

My favorite member of Archie's family is the principal of Riverdale High, good ol' Mr. Weatherbee. He fancies himself Winston Churchill. Every day as he deals with his students, it's blood, sweat, and tears. The Battle of Britain all over again.

In one cartoon Archie has parked a cow in Mr. Weatherbee's office prior to a milking contest at the school festival. Mr. Weatherbee, having been totally stressed out by Archie's antics, sees the cow and assumes he's lost touch with reality. He "knows" that he wouldn't have a cow in his office. When Jughead enters, Mr. Weatherbee's pride automatically creates a cover-up.

How often in a family does pride or

IT TAKES
a
FAMILY

our self-image determine our behavior? Do we go so far as to make fools of ourselves just as comic figures do? Too many times the basic instincts of our human nature can cause trouble in our families. Sometimes, serious trouble.

The Archie family really represents all our families. Sure, there's more action and humor in the comics than we may have in our families, but that's a communicative device to dramatize the story of life. The Archie family is an amalgam of different personalities and perspectives trying to get through each day, and what happens along the way.

Family Thank Tank

1. Do you have a Big Ethel in your family?

_____

_____

_____

_____

_____

2. Who is the most loving member of your family?

_____

_____

_____

_____

_____

_____

Say
Something

IT TAKES
a
FAMILY

Two newlyweds were enjoying the thrill of their first Monday morning "goodbye kiss." It was time for him to come down to earth and leave for work. She would straighten up their new home.

Heading to the office, his thoughts were still at home. Oh, what a gorgeous bride she was. Somehow, through glazed-over eyes, he spotted a colorful parrot in a pet shop window.

What a perfect gift for my darling love bird, he thought.

He quickly ran into the shop, bought the bird, and had it delivered to the love of his life. All day long he felt enormous pride in the gift he sent his beloved. Not only a beautiful bird, but remarkable in that it spoke six languages! He would teach it to say "I love you" in all six, starting that night.

His wife greeted him in an eye-popping outfit and he swept her up in his arms. When the long kiss ended, he took his eyes off her enough to scan the room for the prize bird he had sent. It was nowhere in sight. True, a beautiful table had been set, and she was making romantic conversation, but he didn't notice any

IT TAKES
a
FAMILY

of it. That gallant gesture from the pet shop—the fluent parrot—obsessed him. He wanted to hear her reaction to his gift.

Finally, he could no longer contain himself. "The bird! Where's the bird I sent you?"

"You're eating it," she cooed proudly.

"What? You...you cooked it?"

"Yes, honey. And it took me all day to pluck it."

"But...but that was a prize parrot! It spoke six languages!"

"Well, if it were so smart, why didn't it say something?"

That's an amusing story, but there's a sad truth lurking in the background. Today there's a proud bird that speaks far more than six languages and yet its feathers are being plucked one by one. In this case, a new bride isn't making an innocent mistake. There's a concerted effort by many groups to ground our American eagle.

Our noble emblem that proudly flies over one nation under God should now be on every patriot's endangered species list.

Christians know what it means to come together, to support and to serve.

IT TAKES *a* FAMILY

Recall the words of Galatians 5:1:

> "It is for freedom that Christ has set us free. Stand firm, then, and do not let yourselves be burdened again by a yoke of slavery."

Words to remember. Words to live by.

Those who trust God will mount up with wings as eagles. It's time to mount up, folks. It's time to speak up. Time to look up.

God's spacious skies let eagles soar. The higher they go, the greater their vision. The Psalms tell us that without vision, the nation perishes.

So let our support and applause create the wind beneath those wings. The American eagle has flown in both storm clouds and sunshine since 1776 and still this national symbol represents us in all its proud majesty.

We have a proud heritage. We want to pass it on to our children. When someone attempts to pluck our bird, say something!

Family Thank Tank

1. How long has it been since you sang "God Bless America"?

_____

_____

_____

_____

_____

2. How long has it been since you prayed for our country?

_____

_____

_____

_____

_____

The Facts
of Life

IT TAKES
a
FAMILY

Everyone knows that women give birth to boys and girls. Not many stop to realize that women never give birth to doctors, plumbers, teachers, architects, electricians, and other professionals.

Somewhere between birth and death, these lives make a commitment to become something. They sacrifice, work, and discipline themselves to achieve something and make something of their lives.

No wonder Johann Sebastian Bach was moved to write, "There are three great things in the world—an ocean, a mountain, and a dedicated man or woman."

We listen to a great concert artist perform and marvel at their talent. We'll never know the years of training, the countless sacrifices, and self-discipline that preceded their performance. And we'll never know how many times their parents put their foot down and insisted that music practice come before playing ball.

We sit in a doctor's office and begin fidgeting after a ten-minute wait. We'll never know how long the doctor has waited to keep this appointment with us. College. Medical school. Residency. Internship. Throw in some specialized

IT TAKES
a
FAMILY

training and our doctor has spent more than a dozen years before he or she can examine one hair on our heads.

What about the wizards who keep things running for us? I turn the ignition key and expect electrical, hydraulic, and mechanical miracles to take place under the hood. If those miracles fail to materialize, my fingers know how to walk with purpose through the Yellow Pages.

The innards of every appliance and gadget in our house looks like a display case for Silicon Valley. And yet the young technician takes one look at all those wires, chips, transistors, switches, and gizmos and then repeats the line he or she learned in service school. "Here's your problem!"

Amazing!

The longer I live, the more I realize how dependent I am on others to keep me and the things around me ticking smoothly. And I appreciate the motivation, effort, and expense it took to perfect all the skills we depend on. The company of professionals and tradespeople who are on standby for our emergency calls is another reminder of how large our extended family

IT TAKES a FAMILY

has become.

The point of all this is to focus on the constructive, helpful life, and what it takes to achieve it. It doesn't get much "press," but it's the quality that built our country. There are millions of folks who never make the front page or rate a headline. But they serve on the rescue squads who rush victims to the emergency rooms.

Here's to all the unsung heroes who decided to be someone and to do something for their fellow men and women. We may not be blood relations, but we're brothers and sisters in the spirit. When we need help, they certainly act like family.

Family Thank Tank

1. When was the last time you called for help?

_____

_____

_____

_____

_____

2. Call God. He knows all about your problems, but He wants to hear from you. Ask Him to bless the efforts of those dedicated professionals (list their names here) who can help you.

_____

_____

_____

_____

_____

Kids and Crayons

IT TAKES a FAMILY

Little artists first demonstrate their creativity with crayons. Our great challenge, of course, is to keep that creativity inside the coloring books and not on our walls. Every family has a horror story or two of little darlings expressing themselves in ever-expanding murals.

We don't want to spoil the fun, but sooner or later a basic lesson needs to be taught. As we color a picture, we want to "stay within the lines." The coloring job will be neater and present a much better image if we remember that adage.

What a perfect parable for life. There are perimeters. No matter what stage of life we're playing on, we need to keep within the bounds or we fall off.

In the hands of a child, a crayon helps them learn to draw. It also shows them how to live.

Family Thank Tank

1. Have you gone over any lines lately?

_____

_____

_____

_____

_____

2. Did you know Jesus has an eraser? (See 1 John 1:9.)

_____

_____

_____

_____

_____

Gotcha!

IT TAKES *a* FAMILY

The "last word" is a land mine under any roof where couples fight to get it. Neither party can win. They simply set off an explosion that scars the entire family.

The tongue.

The most powerful muscle in the body. Who can control it? But unless we hold our tongues, we'll never hold our families together.

The Book of James describes it best:

> "Or take ships as an example. Although they are so large and are driven by strong winds, they are steered by a very small rudder wherever the pilot wants to go. Likewise the tongue is a small part of the body, but it makes great boasts. Consider what a great forest is set on fire by a small spark."
>
> James 3:4,5

Consider how a small spark can set a forest on fire. It can consume thousands of acres. Tongues can start brushfires in families, too. And many of us are witnesses to the conflagrations started when

IT TAKES
a
FAMILY

tongues inflame nations.

James makes one other point we should tack to our bulletin boards. The tongue that praises God should not curse men. That's what we call hypocrisy.

Now go back to your Bible, to Ephesians, chapter 4. Paul writes, don't be influenced by deceitfulness. Don't lie. Speak the truth in love. Be kind to one another, tenderhearted, forgiving one another as God in Christ forgave you.

Don't let the sun go down on your anger. Kiss and make up. Forget the last word. Make it three words: "I love you."

Family Thank Tank

1. Will you trust God to help you control your tongue?

_____

_____

_____

_____

_____

2. Will you trust God to help you encourage others?

_____

_____

_____

_____

_____

The Great Healer

IT TAKES *a* FAMILY

Growing children develop so many bumps and bruises, mothers and fathers understandably lose count of the number of kisses they've given to "make it better." As active children grow, they add more than years. They multiply their injuries, and often medicine cabinets don't hold the solutions.

After administering first aid, the wise parent always wraps the wound in prayer. Such prayers teach the child, at a very critical time, that the Great Physician is also the Great Healer. Lessons learned young—when we know we have the child's attention—are lessons that last and are foundational to a solid life. The caregivers who follow this course earn a "Ph.D"—Prayer Heals Dynamically—degree.

My wife and I depended on our "degree" during our son Fred's school days. Once Fred received a head injury during a football game. At the time it only seemed sufficient to take him out of the game. But that night the pain increased and his condition led us to admit him to the hospital.

A specialist diagnosed a severe concus-

IT TAKES
a
FAMILY

sion, but the doctors did not give Fred any medication for pain relief. They didn't want to mask the pain with sedation and thereby impair their diagnosis. They told us our son's condition was a complicated one, and that this was only the beginning.

Fred was in agony for eleven days, during which the doctors tested and observed, unable to give him any effective relief from his pain. When they found blood in his spinal column, they were convinced it came from the brain. They told us that brain surgery was necessary. First, however, they had to perform an angiogram in order to locate the precise point of the bleeding.

Angiogram! I feared the word. My father had gone through the procedure and his account of it would make David Letterman's top ten list of horror stories. Fred knew the story. He'd been through two weeks of constant pain; he had endured all kinds of tests and procedures. He was wrung out.

"Dad, I don't want an angiogram!"

My heart went out to him, but I couldn't ignore the doctor's counsel. What do I say? Do I tell him to be a man, to grit

IT TAKES *a* FAMILY

his teeth, to go through with it?

Every parent can understand the pressure of this situation, but not many could believe the words I suddenly found myself saying. "Fred, we'll pray about this. If God doesn't give you perfect peace, I won't allow the angiogram." Those words came straight out of my mouth—not from my brain.

Obviously, I had gone way out on a limb, in human terms. My son's life was on the line and I was seeking a second opinion—from God. If God didn't respond to this situation, I had placed Fred in even greater jeopardy. But it was inconceivable to me that the Lord, who had revealed Himself to us so clearly in so many ways, was not with us now.

I had a quiet, supreme assurance that He knew all about Fred's condition and that, in His perfect way, He would meet Fred's need.

There, in the middle of a situation that called for anxiety and fear, the One who calmed the waters was in control, and my heart was not troubled. I was at peace, and I trusted Him completely. Was I reckless? Was my head so in the clouds that my feet were not on the ground? As I write about it now, there seems room for that assessment. But at the time it was clear that God was already in the prayer process that was starting. I felt His involvement. He had led me to take action I would never have dared on my own. I couldn't wait to see what He was going to do next.

With that kind of total faith, with no back doors open for escape, Fred and I prayed together, seeking an answer from God. We had an immediate response. The first of many. God sent our assistant pastor into the room and he prayed with us. Within another ten minutes our minister of visitation arrived and he prayed with us. By the time we finished the third prayer within thirty minutes, the Lord's timing and presence were obvious.

"Okay, Dad, I'm ready for the test."

The angiogram should have taken no more than an hour. I paced outside the procedure room for nearly two hours, with no word of his condition. Finally, after nearly three hours, the specialist stepped into the hall.

"Your son is going to be all right."

IT TAKES *a* FAMILY

The team of specialists had run three separate angiograms. I winced at the news that Fred had gone through that painful test three times. The first time, the equipment failed. The second, the doctors were sure they weren't getting accurate readings. The third test confirmed what the doctors couldn't believe. There were no scars, no clots, no evidence whatsoever that there had been any injury or bleeding.

The doctor told me that there was absolutely no medical explanation for Fred's case. But he was healed. I suggested an explanation to the doctor: There is a power and knowledge far beyond that of doctors and technicians. We had been trusting that source of power, and hundreds of believers stood with us in prayer. The doctor smiled.

Meanwhile, our pastor was at home with my wife Hermine. The torment of Fred's constant pain was a heavy load for her and now, with him apparently facing brain surgery, our pastor was preparing Hermine for more serious possibilities. He was telling her that Fred belonged to God. This was Abraham and Isaac all over again. She had to commit her son to God

IT TAKES
a
FAMILY

in faith that His will is best. It required an enormous commitment. As Hermine finished that prayer of commitment, the phone rang. I called with the good news that Fred was going to be okay. From this point on, it was simply a matter of recuperation. The doctors cautioned us that even though Fred's remarkable recovery was complete, we could expect his headaches to continue for about a year. He never had one!

God touched us all during those twenty-one critical days. The most remarkable part of the entire experience was the way God held things together. There was never any sense of panic. His presence was constantly felt as He poured so many acts of love and kindness through those around us.

The greatest act of all took place on the hospital bed. God not only reached down and healed Fred—He took hold of his life.

Fred had made a commitment to Jesus Christ a few years earlier. He went through all the motions of a young Christian—church, Sunday school, youth group, retreats—but things ran much

IT TAKES
a
FAMILY

deeper now. Those white sheets of pain in the hospital had become green pastures. Fred had seen the power of God, face to face. He knew the comfort of Christ in the middle of suffering. Yes, his life had been touched, and now there was no doubt what he would do with it.

Today Fred serves as pastor of a large, growing church just outside Atlanta. He regularly speaks to national audiences and each year makes one overseas trip to address foreign groups. Along the way he's authored eight books.

Do dark clouds have silver linings? Yes, and the lining is another layer of God's silver cord. Take hold of that cord and allow God to weave you into the tapestry of prayer that He's created among His people.

We pray not only for ourselves and our families, we also pray for others in need. And we praise Him for His answers and the special joy of fellowship with others who share our faith and blessings.

Family Thank Tank

1. When was the last time God answered your prayers?

_____

_____

_____

_____

_____

2. Do you have any unanswered prayers?

_____

_____

_____

_____

_____

Capital Idea

IT TAKES
a
FAMILY

"Inside the Beltway" is an epithet that conjures self-serving legislators, elite editors, and bulging bureaucracies. It describes a mindset that doesn't play too well in Peoria. It describes a government out of touch with its citizens.

Hurry! For the sake of our sanity and our view of the future, let's see the true picture. Not many Americans have seen it. We wouldn't have all the problems we have if visitors got past the cherry blossoms and the imposing buildings. Come inside those buildings and be encouraged as I was a few years ago.

My family joined me after I spoke to a convention in our nation's capital. We visited all the national monuments and made an amazing discovery: Scripture is carved inside all those hallowed halls. Yes, in the very city that has legislated God as far out of lives as possible, our leaders are surrounded by constant reminders of what America is really all about. The people who built America gave credit where credit was due.

My family and I took the elevator to the top of the Washington Monument. And then took the stairs down. We

paused on every landing, and it was worth each stop. Every state in the Union submitted a Bible verse to be inscribed—every landing has a verse. "Righteousness exalts a nation." "Blessed is the nation whose God is the Lord." "Jesus said, I am the way, the truth, and the life." What an exhilarating time we had reading the Scriptures as we descended the stairs.

We learned that there is a copper dome on top of the Washington Monument. The words "Praise Be to God" are inscribed on that dome.

We went to the Jefferson Memorial. Inside is a larger-than-life-sized statue of Thomas Jefferson. Carved in the marble wall beside the statue in letters a foot tall is this quote from Jefferson: "God, who gave us life, gave us liberty. Can our liberty survive if we fail to remember it is the gift of God?" It's a quote that ought to be carved in the heart of every elected official who serves us.

The next time you see the House of Representatives on C-Span, look above the Speaker's chair. It says, "In God We Trust," in large letters that no one can miss.

IT TAKES *a* FAMILY

America was founded as a Christian nation. The Pilgrims signed the Mayflower Compact which said,

> "Having undertaken for the glory of God and the advancement of the Christian faith, in the presence of God and one another, we solemnly covenant ourselves together into a civil body politick."

When they landed at Plymouth Rock, William Bradford wrote in his journal,

> "Being thus arrived in a good harbour and brought safe to land, they fell upon their knees and blessed the God of heaven."

On May 19, 1643, the New England Confederation stated, in part,

> "Whereas we all came to America to advance the kingdom of our Lord Jesus Christ, and to enjoy the liberties of the Gospel in purity and peace."

IT TAKES
a
FAMILY

Every colony made similar declarations.

Harvard University was founded to train ministers of the Gospel. In 1776, when America declared its independence, religion and morals accounted for more than 96 percent of school book contents. By 1926, that figure was only 6 percent.

We've certainly come a long way.

The next time you hear a Washington pundit pontificating or see a Beltway insider doing an imitation of a snake-oil salesman, remember our real national heritage. The roots of our country are eternal. The circus is just passing by.

Family Thank Tank

1. Have you thanked God for our godly forefathers?

_____

_____

_____

_____

_____

2. Will you pray for godly leaders today?

_____

_____

_____

_____

_____

Your Vote Counts

IT TAKES *a* FAMILY

God voted for me.

Satan voted against me.

I cast the deciding vote.

Theology doesn't get any plainer than that. The great issue of life can be summed up in three short sentences.

No one can deny that God wants the very best for us. Satan wants the worst. Sounds like an easy choice, doesn't it? We all want the best.

Why is it then that so many people don't even bother to vote? Actually, by not voting, they're voting with Satan.

God says, "He who is not with me is against me," and that's a vote for Satan. He loves it. He doesn't care if you don't vote. In fact, he prefers it that way.

The words to the siren song "My Way" make every ambitious man's heart beat faster, but cardiac arrest produces the same results. Every man who sings that song with feeling is actually singing Satan's song. In truth, if we're not doing it God's way, we're really doing it Satan's way, and he's a tricky puppeteer.

G. K. Chesterton observed that when people cease to believe in God, they end up believing not in nothing, but in any-

IT TAKES *a* FAMILY

thing.

Wherever God has a family of believers, Satan has his machine of unbelievers, feverishly campaigning for your vote. Unfortunately, we have the wrong impression of Satan. Society presents him as a kind of Halloween trick-or-treater, a silly figure in long red underwear with a tail, horns, and pitchfork. He appears a grotesque figure to be laughed at rather than taken seriously. He loves it that way. With a masquerade like that, he's able to cloak his real agenda.

We speak of "raising the devil." We don't have to. He's already up and at 'em. He writes a thousand headlines and dominates the TV news each day.

What's going on in our schools? What's happening to our world? We know we're loaded with symptoms, but what's the disease?

Welcome to Satan's family. Dysfunctional. Bitter. Violent. A cancerous time bomb. Do we want to blow things up, or bring them together?

Welcome to God's family. Love. Joy. Peace. Patience. Kindness. Faithfulness. Self-control.

IT TAKES *a* FAMILY

What a no-brainer. Naturally, we'd choose God's family. But, as humans, we rationalize the decision, and perhaps compromise it here and there. Just change a few details. Nothing important, of course, but we ought to avoid being too rigid.

Do you recognize that voice? That's Satan again. Just open the door a little bit. That's all it takes.

Let's look at the ballot again.

God voted for me.

Satan voted against me.

Whose side are you on? You can't straddle the fence like a spiritual Mugwump with your mug on one side and your wump on the other.

Voting for God is simple. There's no trip to the polling booth. No mailing in an absentee ballot. Simply get down on your knees and make your choice. Remember, you're voting for yourself in this race. The issue is clear. Do you want to be a winner or a loser?

Family Thank Tank

1. Have you thanked God for free choice?

_____

_____

_____

_____

_____

2. Thank Him that He's secured a place for you in heaven, if only you "vote" for Him.

_____

_____

_____

_____

_____

Go With the Flow

IT TAKES *a* FAMILY

Every family seems to be blessed with an inventor, a fix-it fanatic who always has a "better way." Kids especially seem to have unlocked the mysteries of computers, VCRs, and video games., not to mention the workings of fast-food restaurants.

In my family, the patent-pending professor is my nephew. He's only eleven years old but already he has a job upon which the entire fast-food industry exists. He's in charge of "Ketchup Quality Control" for his family. Now this is the very heart of the industry.

Ogden Nash, sort of a Thomas Edison with words, had this apt insight:

"A peculiar thing is the ketchup bottle. First a little, and then a lottle."

Welcome to the world of my nephew. He has unlocked the secret of the ketchup bottle and actually "speeded up" what we know as the fast-food restaurant.

The next time you're at your favorite hamburger haven, notice how smoothly the lines flow. Imagine what it would be like if there were a bottleneck in the

IT TAKES
a
FAMILY

ketchup line. Food would cool and dry out, and tempers would surely flare. (Now, will someone please help me open my ketchup packet?)

While we're on the subject of fast food, and the power of invention, have you heard the one about the submarine sandwich? You might say that one meatball just led to another, but that's only part of the sandwich—I mean story.

One moonlit night in 1942, an Italian submarine slipped into Sicily to on-load supplies. The loaves of bread were so long they had to be taken aboard via the torpedo tubes. Later, at sea, the cook devised a way to relieve the monotony of the long underwater patrols. Instead of cutting the long loaves into the customary slices, he involved the entire crew in his creation. The long loaf was fed through compartment and compartment until it reached the entire length of the submarine. The crewmen were then invited to insert their favorite foods into the loaf. Tomatoes, anchovies, meatballs, salami, cheese, lettuce...any morsel they had in their duffel bags.

The crew sat there in fifty fathoms of

IT TAKES *a* FAMILY

pride, straddling a concoction that has inherited the name "submarine sandwich."

Are you hungry yet? Let's get to the meat of the matter. A family can be considered a *fellowship,* defined as "fellows in the same ship." Sometimes we paddle upstream, and other times we go with the flow. Sometimes it's smooth sailing; sometimes things get rough. Sometimes the captain, or the first mate, or the tiniest stowaway, knows the safest route to port. No matter what the surface conditions, the important thing is that we're paddling in the same direction.

Whether it's a rowboat on a lake, a submarine at Disney World, or a car in the drive-thru lane, we're teammates working together. As a family, we should want to make life better, more fun, and yes, tastier.

Family Thank Tank

1. Do you squeeze as much pleasure out of life as you do ketchup out of the bottle? Have you thanked God for the rich variety of your experiences?

_____

_____

_____

_____

_____

2. What can you do to make things run more smoothly at home?

_____

_____

_____

_____

_____

Appendix

IT TAKES a FAMILY

Affirmations for the Family

*When God is the head
of the house,
everyone is looking
in the same direction.*

IT TAKES
a
FAMILY

Yes, life is full of mystery.
That's why families are essential.

The very first "church" that God formed
was the family.

No matter where God puts us,
we can take hold of our children
and lift them up to see
the enchantment and adventure of life.

A gumdrop is often more valuable
than a five-carat diamond.

God's family is priceless.

Noah never built an ark before,
but he did it.
He never rode the world's first round-up
before, but he did it.
He never saw such a storm before,
but he got through it.

The tides of this world come and go.
And God parts water when He has to.

IT TAKES *a* FAMILY

God wants your life to overflow
with His love; He knows every family
has room for more.

Every family should make God
their top priority.

Instead of teaching a child
to *do* something, let's teach him
to *be* something.

Without that assurance of love,
a child feels they're not worth much.

Obedience comes from respect,
and respect is caught much easier
than it's taught.

No matter how large or small the family,
a child needs to know he belongs.

Walls will never be high enough
or strong enough to contain the rage
that grows without a parent's love
and involvement.

The worst virus to spread in our homes
is neglect.

IT TAKES
a
FAMILY

Whatever metaphor fits the situation,
God will provide the metamorphosis.

Accept each other as Christ accepts us—
just as we are.

We belong to each other
and we need each other.
No matter how high the wall between
you and a loved one, no matter how wide
the chasm, hold on and pray.
God doesn't divide: He multiplies.

God has a very special set of lyrics,
just for you.

Until we get to heaven,
none of us will ever know
all the prayers that have been said
on our behalf.

Forget the last word.
Make it three words: "I love you."

After administering first aid,
the wise parent always wraps
the wound in prayer.

Affirmations for Men and Fathers

*Great men are they
who see that the spiritual
is stronger than
any material force.*

Ralph Waldo Emerson

IT TAKES
a
FAMILY

Only be thou strong
and very courageous, that thou mayest
observe to do according to all the
law...turn not from it to the right hand
or to the left, that thou mayest prosper
whithersoever thou goest.
Joshua 1:7 KJV

The just man walketh in his integrity:
his children are blessed after him.
Proverbs 20:7 KJV

It is a wise father
that knows his own child.
William Shakespeare

Husbands, love your wives,
just as Christ loved the church
and gave himself up for her.
Ephesians 5:25

An honest man's the noblest work
of God.
Alexander Pope

O Lord, let us not live to be useless,
for Christ's sake.
John Wesley

IT TAKES *a* FAMILY

This is what a father ought to be about:
helping his son to form the habit
of doing right on his own initiative,
rather than because he's afraid
of some serious consequence.
Terence (160 B.C.)

One other thing stirs me when I look
back at my youthful days, the fact that so
many people gave me something or were
something to me without knowing it.
Albert Schweitzer

Lo, children are an heritage
of the LORD:
and the fruit of the womb
is his reward.
Psalm 127:3 KJV

No man has ever lived that had enough,
Of children's gratitude or woman's love.
William Butler Yeats

There is no more lovely, friendly
and charming relationship, communion,
or company than a good marriage.
Martin Luther

IT TAKES
a
FAMILY

"But while he was still a long way off,
his father saw him and was filled
with compassion for him;
he ran to his son, threw his arms
around him and kissed him."
Luke 15:20

If God is for us, who can be against us?
Romans 8:31b

Blessed is the man who perseveres
under trial, because when he has stood
the test, he will receive the crown of life
that God has promised to those
who love him.
James 1:12

One man with courage makes a majority.
Andrew Jackson

For God did not give us a spirit
of timidity, but a spirit of power,
of love and of self-discipline.
2 Timothy 1:7

Every generation revolts against its fathers
and makes friends with its grandfathers.
Lewis Mumford

IT TAKES *a* FAMILY

That our sons may be as plants
grown up in their youth;
that our daughters may be as corner-
stones, polished after the similitude
of a palace...yea, happy is that people
whose God is the LORD.
Psalm 144:12, 15b KJV

One on God's side is a majority.
Wendell Phillips

Unless the LORD builds the house,
its builders labor in vain.
Psalm 127:1a

...Choose you this day whom ye will
serve;...but as for me and my house,
we will serve the LORD.
Joshua 24:15 KJV

Fathers, do not exasperate your children;
instead, bring them up in the training
and instruction of the Lord.
Ephesians 6:4

If you don't crack the shell,
you can't eat the nut.
Russian proverb

IT TAKES
a
FAMILY

Endure hardship as discipline;
God is treating you as sons.
For what son is not disciplined
by his father?
Hebrews 12:7

That is why, for Christ's sake,
I delight in weaknesses, in insults,
in hardships, in persecutions,
in difficulties. For when I am weak,
then I am strong.
2 Corinthians 12:10

Finally, brothers, whatever is true,
whatever is noble, whatever is right,
whatever is pure, whatever is lovely,
whatever is admirable—
if anything is excellent or praiseworthy—
think about such things.
Philippians 4:8

He that can't endure the bad,
will not live to see the good.
Yiddish proverb

Affirmations for Women and Mothers

What have I to ask beside?
Can I doubt
His tender mercy,
Who through life
has been my Guide?
Fanny Crosby

IT TAKES
a
FAMILY

Her children arise up,
and call her blessed; her husband also,
and he praiseth her.
Proverbs 31:28 KJV

There is in every true woman's heart
a spark of heavenly fire, which lies
dormant in the broad daylight
of prosperity, but which kindles up
and beams and blazes
in the dark hour of adversity.
Washington Irving

When we do the best that we can,
we never know what miracle is wrought
in our life, or in the life of another.
Helen Keller

A rich child often sits
in a poor mother's lap.
Danish proverb

Who can find a virtuous woman?
for her price is far above rubies.
Proverbs 31:10 KJV

IT TAKES *a* FAMILY

The aged women...be in behaviour
as becometh holiness, not false accusers,
not given to much wine, teachers of good
things; That they may teach the young
women to be sober, to love their
husbands, to love their children.
Titus 2:3-4 KJV

For whosoever shall do the will
of my Father which is in heaven,
the same is my brother, and sister,
and mother.
Matthew 12:50 KJV

Favour is deceitful, and beauty is vain:
but a woman that feareth the LORD,
she shall be praised.
Proverbs 31:30 KJV

No man is poor
who has had a Godly mother.
Abraham Lincoln

And Jacob served seven years for Rachel;
and they seemed unto him but a few
days, for the love he had to her.
Genesis 29:20 KJV

IT TAKES
a
FAMILY

I have been reminded of your sincere
faith, which first lived in your
grandmother Lois and in your mother
Eunice and, I am persuaded,
now lives in you also.
2 Timothy 1:5

There are two ways of spreading light:
to be the candle
or the mirror that reflects it.
Edith Wharton

All the privilege I claim for my own
sex...is that of loving longest,
when existence or when hope is gone.
Jane Austen

The greatest love is a mother's;
then come a dog's; then comes
a sweetheart's.
Polish proverb

She opens her arms to the poor and
extends her hands to the needy.
When it snows, she has no fear
for her household; for all of them
are clothed in scarlet.
Proverbs 31:20-21

IT TAKES *a* FAMILY

A wife of noble character is her husband's
crown, but a disgraceful wife
is like decay in his bones.
Proverbs 12:4

Who ran to help me when I fell,
And would some pretty story tell,
Or kiss the place to make it well?
My mother.
Ann Taylor (1804)

A mother is not a person to lean on,
but a person to make leaning
unnecessary.
Dorothy Canfield Fisher

Every wise woman buildeth her house:
but the foolish plucketh it down
with her hands.
Proverbs 14:1 KJV

Of all the rights of women,
the greatest is to be a mother.
Lin Yutang

As one whom his mother comforteth,
so will I comfort you....
Isaiah 66:13 KJV

IT TAKES
a
FAMILY

Greet Priscilla and Aquila,
my fellow workers in Christ Jesus.
They risked their lives for me.
Not only I but all the churches of the
Gentiles are grateful to them.
Romans 16:3

An ideal wife is any woman
who has an ideal husband.
Booth Tarkington

Life is made up of sobs, sniffles, and
smiles, with sniffles predominating.
O. Henry

A woman when she is in travail
hath sorrow, because her hour is come:
but as soon as she is delivered of the child
she remembereth no more the anguish,
for joy that a man is born into the world.
John 16:21 KJV

Those who are really in earnest
must be willing to be anything
or nothing in the world's estimation.
Susan Brownell Anthony

IT TAKES a FAMILY

The inhabitants of the villages ceased,
they ceased in Israel, until that I Deborah
arose, that I arose a mother in Israel.
Judges 5:7 KJV

Behold the handmaid of the Lord;
be it unto me according to thy word.
Luke 1:38 KJV

As a jewel of gold in a swine's snout, so is
a fair woman which is without discretion.
Proverbs 11:22 KJV

The soul can split the sky in two,
And let the face of God shine through.
Edna St. Vincent Millay